The Student's Guide to Writing Economics

Economists bring clear thinking and a host of analytical techniques to a wide range of topics. *The Student's Guide to Writing Economics* will equip students with the tools and skills required to write accomplished essays.

Robert Neugeboren provides a concise and accessible guide to the writing process taking the student through the stages of planning, revising, and editing pieces of work. This book presents the core principles of the "economics approach" and covers essential topics such as:

- the key to successful writing in economics
- basic methods economists use to analyze data and communicate ideas
- suggestions for finding and focusing your chosen topic
- vital techniques for researching topics
- how to approach the citing of sources and creating a bibliography

The Student's Guide to Writing Economics also includes up-to-date appendices covering fields in economics, standard statistical sources, online search engines, and electronic indices to periodical literature.

This guide will prove an invaluable resource for students seeking to understand how to write successfully in economics.

Robert Neugeboren is Lecturer in Economics and Assistant Director of Undergraduate Studies at Harvard University, USA.

The Student's Guide to Writing Economics

Robert Neugeboren

Routledge
Taylor & Francis Group

NEW YORK AND LONDON

First published 2005
by Routledge
270 Madison Ave, New York, NY 10016

Simultaneously published in the UK
by Routledge
2 Park Square, Milton Park, Abingdon, Oxon OX14 4RN

Routledge is an imprint of the Taylor & Francis Group

Typeset in Perpetua and Bell Gothic by
Book Now Ltd
Printed and bound in Great Britain by
TJ International Ltd, Padstow, Cornwall

British Library Cataloguing in Publication Data
A catalogue record for this book is available from the British Library

Library of Congress Cataloging in Publication Data
Neugeboren, Robert
The student's guide to writing economics / Robert Neugeboren.
      p. cm.
Includes bibliographical references and index.
    1. English language–Rhetoric–Problems, exercises, etc. 2.
Economics–Authorship–Problems, exercises, etc. 3. Academic
writing–Problems, exercises, etc. I. Title.
PE1479.E35.N48   2005
808'.06633–dc22   2005005272

ISBN10: 0–415–70122–8 (hbk)
ISBN10: 0–415–70123–6 (pbk)

ISBN13: 9–78–0–415–70122–8 (hbk)
ISBN13: 9–78–0–415–70123–5 (pbk)

Contents

Contributors

CHRISTOPHER FOOTE is Senior Economist in the Research Department at the Federal Reserve Bank of Boston. From 1996 to 2002, he taught at Harvard University's Department of Economics, where he also served as Director of Undergraduate Studies. In July 2002, he accepted a position as senior staff economist with the Council of Economic Advisers, becoming chief economist at CEA in February 2003. He joined the Boston Fed in October 2003.

MIREILLE JACOBSON is Assistant Professor of Planning, Policy, and Design at the School of Social Ecology at the University of California. In 2001, she earned a doctorate in economics from Harvard University, where she was a National Science Foundation Graduate Fellow. She is currently a Robert Wood Johnson Foundation Scholar in Health Policy Research at the University of Michigan.

KERRY WALK is Director of the Princeton Writing Program. Before leaving Harvard University in 2001, she was Assistant Director of the Harvard Writing Project, which seeks to enhance the role of writing in courses and departments campus-wide. Walk has given faculty workshops on assigning and responding to student writing at institutions across the country. She received her Ph.D. in English from the University of California, Berkeley.

Acknowledgments

This guide was developed in conjunction with the Economics Tutorial Program at Harvard University, with support and assistance from The Harvard Writing Project. Nancy Sommers, Sosland Director of Expository Writing, proposed the idea in 1999, and I was asked to write the guide, which has since been distributed to the sophomores in the department each year. Kerry Walk, then Assistant Director of the Writing Project, saw the project through from inception to completion, commented on drafts, gave advice at every stage, and ultimately added the section on "Formatting and documentation" (Chapter 5). Christopher Foote, then Assistant Professor of Economics and Director of Undergraduate Studies, wrote part of Chapter 4, and Mireille Jacobson made substantial contributions to the section on "Writing economically" (Chapter 1), and she compiled the original appendices. Oliver Hart, Michael Murray, Lorenzo Isla, Tuan Min Li, Allison Morantz, and Stephen Weinberg also gave very helpful comments. Rajiv Shankar updated the appendices and prepared the manuscript for printing. Special thanks to Anita Mortimer, with regrets for her recent passing.

Introduction: The economic approach

Economists study everything from money and prices to child rearing and the environment. They analyze small-scale decision-making and large-scale international policy-making. They compile data about the past and make predictions about the future. Many economic ideas have currency in everyday life, cropping up in newspapers, magazines, and policy debates. The amount you pay every month to finance a car or new home purchase will depend on interest rates. Business people make investment plans based on expectations of future demand, and policy-makers devise budgets to achieve a desired macroeconomic equilibrium.

While the range of topics that interest economists is vast, there is a unique approach to knowledge, something common to the way all economists see the world. Economists share certain assumptions about how the economy works, and they use standard methods for analyzing data and communicating their ideas. The purpose of this guide is to help you to think and write like an economist.

ECONOMICS AND THE PROBLEM OF SCARCITY

Since its beginnings as "the dismal science," economics has been preoccupied with the problem of scarcity. The hours in a day, the money in one's pocket, the food the earth can supply are all limited; spending resources on one activity necessarily comes at the expense of some other, foregone opportunity. Scarcity provides economics with its central problem: how to make choices in the context of constraint.

Accordingly, economists ask questions such as: How does a consumer choose a bundle of commodities, given her income and prices? How does a country choose to meet its objectives, given its national budget? How do decision-makers allocate scarce resources among alternative activities with different uses?

While this central economic problem may be rather narrow, the range of topics that interest economists is vast. Indeed, insofar as it can be characterized as choice under constraint, any kind of behavior falls within the scope of economic analysis. As Lord Lionel Robbins (1984), one of the great economists of the twentieth century, put it:

> We do not say that the production of potatoes is economic activity and the production of philosophy is not. We say rather that, in so far as either kind of activity involves the relinquishment of other desired alternatives, it has its economic aspect. There are no limitations on the subject matter of Economic Science save this.

It should come as no surprise that economists are sometimes called "imperialists" by other social scientists for their encroachment on fields that traditionally belong to other disciplines. For instance, historians studying the migration patterns of eighteenth-century European peasants have explained the movement out of the countryside and into the cities in terms of broad social and cultural factors: the peasants were subjects of changing times, swept along by the force of history. By contrast, economists, such as Samuel L. Popkin (1979), have attributed urban migration patterns to the trade-offs faced and choices made by individual agents; from this perspective, the peasants' behavior was rational.

THE ASSUMPTION OF RATIONALITY

Economists approach a wide range of topics with the assumption that the behavior under investigation is best understood as if it were rational (though we know that not all behavior is, in fact, rational) and that the best explanations, models, and theories we construct take rationality as the norm. Rationality, in the words of Frank Hahn, is the "weak causal proposition" that sets all economic analyses in motion. "Economics can be distinguished from other social sciences by the belief that most (all?) behavior can be explained by assuming that agents have stable, well-defined preferences and make rational choices consistent with those preferences" (Colin Camerer and Richard Thaler, 1995).

Rationality, in the standard sense of the economist, means that agents prefer more of what they want to less. This may seem like a rather strong proposition, insofar as it seems to imply that human behavior is necessarily calculated and self-interested. But the assumption of rationality does not imply anything about the content of agents' wants, or preferences; hence to be rational is not necessarily to be selfish. One can want others to be better off and rationally pursue this objective as well. Economists assume that whatever their preferences, agents will attempt to maximize their satisfaction subject to the constraints they face. And good economics

3

writing will take the assumption of rational behavior as its starting point.

THE THEORY OF INCENTIVES

The theory of incentives posits that individual agents, firms, or people, make decisions by comparing costs and benefits. When costs or benefits – the constraints on choices – change, behavior may also change. In other words, agents respond to incentives.

Many recent developments in economics and public policy are based on the theory of incentives. For example, recent welfare reforms recognize that traditional welfare, which guarantees a basic level of income but is taken away once that level is surpassed, provides incentives for those below the earnings threshold to stay out of the formal workforce. This and other criticisms have led to the adoption and expansion of programs such as the Earned Income Tax Credit (EITC). The EITC seeks to rectify this particular incentive problem by making transfers only to working individuals. Such policy changes suggest that incentives matter for behavior. Thus, a thorough analysis of any behavior, and a well-written account of it, must account for incentive effects.

TYPES OF WRITING ASSIGNMENTS

Depending on the course, the instructor, and the degree to which writing has been integrated into the curriculum, there are several types of writing assignments you might see. Some courses will sequence their assignments, working on basic skills in short assignments and building to a longer term paper. No matter what the format, length, etc., it is important to understand the assignment's goal or purpose.

Response paper (1–2pp)

Response papers might involve summarizing an assigned reading or answering a specific set of questions about the text. Instructors use these to focus your attention on important topics and to stimulate class discussion. Response papers can also help develop the themes and vocabulary needed for writing successful longer papers.

Short essay (3–4pp)

Short essays may require you to analyze two articles and compare their policy implications, explain a model, criticize an argument, present a case study, evaluate an intellectual debate, and so on. A short essay differs from a response paper in that it will usually ask you to have a thesis, or central argument, and then present some kind of analysis to make your case.

Empirical exercise (5–6pp)

Often courses will assign an empirical exercise in which you are asked to analyze economic data using a standard statistical software package (e.g., Stata, Minitab, SAS, SPSS, etc.). An empirical exercise will give you experience in answering an economic question with data and drawing conclusions from evidence.

Term paper (10–15pp)

The term paper addresses a topic in depth and combines skills developed throughout the semester. It typically includes a literature review, an empirical component, a discussion of results, and perhaps a discussion of policy implications. It may build on earlier short assignments, including a prospectus, in which you will propose a thesis or question and detail how the issue will be addressed. The term paper may require research beyond what has been assigned to the class.

Make sure you clear up any confusion about the assignment by asking your instructor specific questions about what he or she is looking for. The earlier you get clarification, the better able you will be to complete the assignment (and get a good grade). For longer papers, you may want to hand in rough drafts. Getting feedback may improve your writing considerably and generally makes for more interesting papers.

PLAN OF THIS GUIDE

Understanding the way economists see the world is a necessary step on the way to good economics writing. Chapter 1 describes the keys you need to succeed as a writer of economics and offers an overview of the writing process from beginning to end. Chapter 2 describes the basic methods economists use to analyze data and communicate their ideas. Chapter 3 offers suggestions for finding and focusing your topic, including standard economic sources and techniques for doing economic research. Chapter 4 tells you how to write a term paper. Finally, Chapter 5 provides a guide to citing sources and creating a bibliography. Three appendices provide useful information for developing your term papers. Appendix A provides a roadmap of fields in economics and can help define very broad areas of interest. Appendix B presents an overview of economics resources on the Internet, with a brief directory of useful websites and links to statistical sources that you may wish to use for your own research. Appendix C lists the relevant electronic indices to periodical literature, invaluable resources for the initial stages of any paper.

Chapter 1

Writing economically

LIST OF SUB-TOPICS

- Overview of the writing process
- Getting started
- The keys to good economics writing
- Achieving clarity
- Managing your time

Pick up any publication of the American Economics Association and you will discover a few things about writing economics. First, the discourse is often mathematical, with lots of formulas, lemmas, and proofs. Second, writing styles vary widely. Some authors are very dry and technical; a few are rather eloquent.

You do not have to be a great "writer" to produce good economics writing. This is because economics writing is different from many other types of writing. It is essentially technical writing, where the goal is not to turn a clever phrase, hold the reader in suspense, or create multi-layered nuance, but rather to achieve clarity. Elegant prose is nice, but clarity is the only style that is relevant for our purposes. A clear presentation will allow the strength of your underlying analysis and the quality of your research to shine through.

OVERVIEW OF THE WRITING PROCESS

If you have ever pulled an all-nighter and done reasonably well on the assignment, you may be tempted to rely on your ability to churn out pages of prose late at night. This is not a sensible strategy. Good economics papers just do not "happen" without time spent on preparation; you cannot hide a lack of research, planning, and revising behind cleverly constructed prose. More time will produce better results, though returns to effort will be diminishing at some point. Here, too, the principles of economy apply.

GETTING STARTED

Getting started is often the hardest part of writing. The blank page or screen can bring on writer's block, and sustaining an argument through many pages can seem daunting, particularly when you know your work will be graded. Do not let these concerns paralyze you; break the paper down into smaller parts, and get started on the simpler tasks. Economics writing usually requires a review of the relevant literature (more on this later). Especially if you are stuck, this can be a great way to begin.

THE KEYS TO GOOD ECONOMICS WRITING

Writing in economics, as in any academic discipline, is never simply a matter of asserting your opinions. While your ideas are important, your job includes establishing your credentials as a writer of economics, by demonstrating your knowledge of economic facts and theories, identifying and interpreting the underlying economic models, understanding what others have said about the relevant issues, evaluating the available evidence, and presenting a persuasive

argument. Even if you do not write particularly well, you can produce good economics papers by attending to three basic tasks:

Research

Economic research generally entails three stages. First, you may
need to gain a broad overview of your topic: start from a text book
on the subject, or discover what resources are available in that field
over the internet (see Appendix B1). Second, you may need to
review the literature on the topic: simple or exhaustive searches can
be made through online academic search portals which will find
perhaps hundreds of articles based on your narrow search criteria
(see Appendix C). Sometimes the entire article is available online;
usually at least an abstract is given, and you have to manually locate
the article in your library, or get it via inter-library loan. Third, even
if you are referring to only a single paper, you may need to update
some of the relevant statistics, or collect and analyze substantial data
on your own, which you can get from any of a number of standard
statistical sources (see Appendix B2). In general, your writing
will reflect the quality of your research, and good writing will
demonstrate that you understand the findings that are relevant to
your topic.

Organization

Once you have found your sources, you will need to organize your
ideas and outline your paper. Economists usually organize their
writing by using simplified models (such as supply and demand,
cost/benefit analysis, and comparative advantage). Therefore, a
literature review is often followed by the presentation of a model,
usually one of the standard models or, for the theoretically inclined,
one of your own devising. Models are used to organize data and
generate hypotheses about how some aspect of the economy works.

Analysis

Reducing something complex into simpler parts is an integral part of economic rigor. Statistical analysis (or econometrics) takes vast piles of data and returns useful numerical summaries that can be used to test various economic models and make predictions about the future. Mathematics is very helpful here because it is a precise language that can articulate the way basic economic relations are conceptualized, measured, and defined. Nonetheless, even before you have mastered sophisticated statistical and mathematical techniques, your goals should be writing clearly, following a line of deductive reasoning to its conclusion, and applying the rules of inference correctly. These are the marks of good economics writing.

AN EXAMPLE FROM THE LITERATURE

Generally, in the first few paragraphs of a paper, economists set up their research question as well as the model and data they use to think about it. This style can be useful to both writer and reader as it establishes the structure of the work that follows. Unfortunately, it sometimes means a stilted or dry presentation. An excerpt from a piece by two of the field's most eloquent authors, Claudia Goldin and Lawrence F. Katz (1996), illustrates a skilful approach to setting up a research question, placing it in the literature, and outlining how the work to follow extends existing research. Notice, in particular, that these steps need not be completely independent.

The piece, taken from the authors' work on the historical relationship among technology, human capital, and the wage structure, starts by presenting the facts motivating the question:

Recent technological advances and a widening of the wage structure have led many to conclude that technology and human capital are relative complements. The possibility that such a relationship exists today has prompted a widely held conjecture that technology and skill have always been relative complements.

Next they explain the existing theories behind this relationship:

According to this view, technological advance always serves to widen the wage structure, and only large injections of education slow its relentless course. A related literature demonstrates that capital and skill are relative complements today and in the recent past (Zvi Griliches, 1969). Thus capital deepening appears also to have increased the relative demand for the educated, serving further to stretch the wage structure.

Then they clearly and simply state their question:

Physical capital and technology are now regarded as the relative complements of human capital, but have they been so for the past two centuries?

Next they cite more of the related literature:

Some answers have already been provided. A literature has emerged on the bias to technological change across history that challenges the view that physical capital and human capital have always been relative complements.

Finally they propose how they seek to answer this question:

We argue that capital–skill complementarity was manifested in the aggregate economy as particular technologies spread, specifically batch and continuous process methods of production.

Their paper goes on to establish the empirical evidence that backs up this assertion. As evidenced by the example above, the clarity of your prose, the quality of your research, the organization of your argument, and the rigor of your analysis are the keys to your success as an economics writer.

ACHIEVING CLARITY

Clear writing is easy to read but hard to write. It rarely occurs without considerable effort and a willingness to revise and rework. As McCloskey (1985), the dean of economics writing, tells us: "it is good to be brief in the whole essay and in the single word, during the midnight fever of composition and during the morning chill of revision." The rules of clear writing apply to the organization of the entire paper, to the order of paragraphs, to sentences, and to words.

Clarity can be achieved in stages:

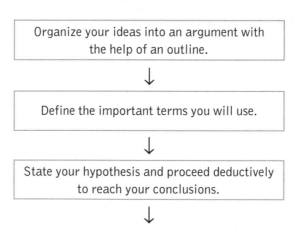

Organize your ideas into an argument with the help of an outline.

↓

Define the important terms you will use.

↓

State your hypothesis and proceed deductively to reach your conclusions.

↓

> Avoid excess verbiage.

> Edit yourself, remove what is not needed, and keep revising until you get down to a simple, efficient way of communicating.

This last stage is crucial. Take, for example, the following excerpt from a student's short response paper:

> In the beginning of the 1980s, the problem of homelessness in the United States became apparent (Richard B. Freeman and Brian Hall, 1989). Since then, the number of homeless in this country has continued to grow. While the problem of homelessness, in itself, is obviously a problem that is quite relevant to other fields of economic study, it has also given rise to a phenomenon that is an interesting topic for the study of behavioral economics: the donation of money to help the homeless population.

With a little revision, the author could have achieved a more clear and concise introduction:

> Early in the 1980s, increasing homelessness in the United States became apparent (Freeman and Hall, 1989). Since then, the number of homeless has continued to grow. While homelessness is studied in many fields of economics, it has given rise to a particular phenomenon – the donation of money directly to the homeless – that interests behavioral economists in particular.

13

Below are some additional tips to achieving clarity and some examples that apply them. These and many other useful tips can be found in Strunk and White (1979), Turabian (1996), and Gibaldi (2003).

Use the active voice

It turns a weak statement (first one) into a more direct assertion (second statement):

> In this paper, the effect of centralized wage-setting institutions on the industry distribution of employment is studied.
>
> This paper studies the effect of centralized wage-setting institutions on the industry distribution of employment.

Put statements in positive form

> Many day-traders did not pay attention to the warnings of experts.

This statement is more concisely conveyed as follows:

> Many day-traders ignored the warnings of experts.

Omit needless words

> In spite of the fact that the stock market is down, many experts feel that financial markets may perform reasonably well this quarter.

A better way to express the same thing is:

> Although the stock market is down, financial markets may still perform reasonably well this quarter.

In summaries, generally stick to one tense

> This study showed that dividend payouts increase when dividend income was less tax-disadvantaged relative to capital gains.

An improvement uses the present tense throughout:

> This study shows that dividend payouts increase when dividend income is less tax-disadvantaged relative to capital gains.

Few writers achieve clarity without continual editing. Once you have your basic ideas down, be sure to reread and revise your work.

MANAGING YOUR TIME

The best laid plans for writing a good paper can be wrecked by poor time management. Make sure you clear up any confusion about the assignment right away. Set deadlines for completing each phase of the project:

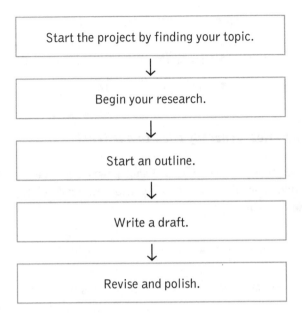

Divide your time, from the moment you receive your assignment to the moment it is due, into segments allotted to each task. Hold yourself to the deadlines you set, and allow yourself time to revise and polish the paper. The payoff will be a better product, a better grade, and less anxiety throughout.

Chapter 2

The language of economic analysis

LIST OF SUB-TOPICS

- Economic models
- Hypothesis testing
- Improving the fit
- Applying the tools

The economy is a complex web of interdependent elements, and understanding any part is a significant accomplishment. The price of tea in the USA is determined by many factors, including individual preferences (or tastes), labor costs, weather conditions, and the price of tea in China, among others. Preferences, labor costs, weather, etc., are in turn connected to other factors, including the price of coffee, which in turn can affect the price of tea. All the parts can be moving simultaneously, making it hard to see what is causing what.

To write effectively about economics, you have to understand how economists think about such complicated phenomena. In general, to make their task easier, economists focus on and try to isolate simple causal connections, often between two variables *ceteris paribus*, or "other things being equal." "Other things being equal," what is the effect of a change in labor costs on the price of tea? "Other things being equal," how does a change in the price of coffee affect the price of tea?

This kind of analysis allows economists to say something very precise about well-defined relationships and to run rigorous tests to measure the strength and direction of their connections. Of course, focusing on just one relationship at a time means other relationships are artificially held constant, so that our analyses necessarily diverge from reality. They are hypothetical. But simplification and abstraction are necessary ingredients of any theoretical enterprise, and a good economist knows the real world is more complex.

ECONOMIC MODELS

Economic analysis is characterized by the use of models, simplified representations of how economic phenomena work. Supply and demand, cost/benefit analysis, and comparative advantage are examples of basic economic models. A model is a theory rendered in precise, usually mathematical, terms. Economists build models the way curious scientists do: Reduce the phenomenon to its basic elements and recombine these elements so as to produce a model that resembles the original in relevant respects. Take it apart, figure out how it works, then put it back together and see if it goes.

Economic models specify relationships between two kinds of variables: *exogenous variables* and *endogenous variables* (Gregory N. Mankiw, 1997). Exogenous variables are inputs to the model, factors that influence what happens but are themselves determined "outside" the model. They are givens, fixed values that are assumed not to change over the period of analysis. Endogenous variables are outputs of the model, determined "within." Usually, a mathematical function is used to represent the relationship between exogenous and endogenous variables. Systems of relationships, in which changes in one part of the economy have different consequences in others, are often conveniently represented by systems of functions. For example, we can model the market for ice cream in terms of three functions:

The quantity of ice cream demanded depends (negatively) on the price of ice cream and (positively) on income (Y): $Q_d = D(P_I, Y)$

The quantity of ice cream supplied depends (negatively) on the price of milk (because ice cream is made from milk) and on the price of ice cream: $Q_s = S(P_I, P_M)$

In equilibrium, the quantity of ice cream supplied equals the quantity demanded: $Q_d = Q_s$

In this model, the price of milk and the level of income are exogenous variables; the price of ice cream and the quantity of ice cream exchanged are endogenous variables. By plugging data (exogenous variables) into the model, it is possible to predict the behavior of the endogenous variables, thus generating hypotheses about phenomena that have not yet been observed.

Applying basic models allows one to make predictions about the real world economy, both forward-looking predictions about, say, future interest rates and backward-looking predictions about, say, the savings rate during the Depression. Models also provide guidance about where to look for and how to look at data, and they provide a structure on which the rest of the paper can hang.

HYPOTHESIS TESTING

A model's predictions about the future or the past are essentially empirical hypotheses: claims, supported by facts, about how some economic phenomenon works. Most economists, aspiring to be good social scientists, would like to test their hypotheses under laboratory conditions. But this is not ordinarily possible. Instead, we take sample data from the real world, by looking at census reports, balance sheets and the like, and we use statistical methods to test the predictive power of our models and the hypotheses they generate.

Most economic data come in, or can be easily transformed into, numerical terms. Prices and quantities are numbers, and economists also attach numerical measurements to factors such as standards of living that do not usually come in quantified form. But a long list of numbers is just that until a relationship among them can be specified that imparts some order. By building and using models, economists are able to focus on simple, sometimes subtle, relationships in the data and explain the causal links involved. Finding the pattern in the data allows one to say something about how the economy works. A set of well-known models can greatly simplify the task of organizing and communicating your ideas. But the real test of a model is how well it helps us understand the workings of the economy.

 AN EXAMPLE: REGRESSION

Say, for instance, you are interested in explaining the causes of inflation. You study the literature and learn about a connection between the level of economic activity and the level of inflation. You formulate a simple hypothesis:

Hypothesis: High levels of employment lead to high levels of inflation.

Observations: Monthly employment (X) and inflation rates (Y) in the US from 1980–1995. (Two lists of $12 \times 16 = 192$ observations.)

Regression: $Y = a + bX + c$. b measures the correlation between X and Y. If b is positive and statistically significant, the hypothesis cannot be rejected. (a is a constant; c is an error term.)

In order to run such a regression you will need a fairly large number of observations. Without enough data you may not be able to decide between this and the alternative, or null, hypothesis (i.e., high levels of employment have no relationship to high levels of inflation) by statistical measures alone. In such cases, there may be better ways to do an empirical exercise (e.g., case study; experimental methods).

Even with enough data, statistical analyses show correlation, not causation. A *model* is needed to explain *how* things work – for instance, how high levels of employment lead to high levels of inflation.

IMPROVING THE FIT

The fit between a model and reality is never perfect. When the fit is good, we can make better predictions about the future and better understand the past. In the former case, the passage of time will fail to disconfirm the prediction; in the latter case, historical research will match our expectations. As in any science, our theories can really only be disproved. However, when our predictions are correct, the weight we place on our models increases. When our predictions are wrong, we are left either looking for more data or

21

perhaps a new or revised model. That model may be used to generate new predictions, which can then be confronted with new data, which may again bring disconfirmation of the prediction and suggest a revision of the current model.

APPLYING THE TOOLS

Most of the writing done in economics involves the application of old models to new data, with the goal of better understanding some real world economic phenomenon. This may or may not involve analyzing a large dataset. This example applies economic tools – namely, game theoretic analysis – to one particular issue, the role of international institutions in the post-Cold War era:

> The purpose of this paper is to discuss the continuing role of NATO and the likelihood of lasting cooperation among the organization's member states in a post-Cold War world. Game theory and the study of strategic interactions, although initially devised as a tool for understanding Cold War motives and actions, nevertheless are extremely applicable to a post-Cold War environment. I therefore plan to incorporate several relevant international relations issues into a game theoretical perspective – first to discuss the cooperation that actually occurred in NATO since the 1940s, and then to explain why similar cooperation may be unlikely among security-based regimes after the collapse of the Soviet Union.

Another kind of writing, the *theory paper*, involves criticizing the models we use and proposing better ones. The goal of the theory paper is to improve the conceptual underpinnings of the particular analytical tools we use to understand the actual economy. This may be a better model of how firms behave in uncertain market conditions, or a new way to measure the level of national economic activity, or a synthesis of existing theories to produce a new, more general theory.

Because all economic models are crude approximations of a complex world, it is necessary to assess just how crude the approximations are before we can say which model better fits the data. Interpreting statistics and determining what can and cannot be reliably inferred given the observations available requires knowledge of economic theory as well as a healthy dose of mathematics. Mathematical logic is also used to build new models, both to formalize the logical structure of the model and to test for its coherence and internal consistency. The mathematics of model building does not involve numbers, but it does specify quantities (quantifiers) and uses well-defined operators to combine (sets of) propositions.

Economic theory was not always so mathematical. And the mathematization of economic theory has had costs as well as benefits. The benefits are that, in many cases, more can be said quickly and precisely, because mathematics is a powerful language and convenient shorthand. The cost is that not all relevant phenomena are easily cast in mathematical terms or can be only crudely captured mathematically. Another cost is that economic theory becomes somewhat less accessible to students and to the world at large, in which public policy debates are conducted.

Chapter 3

Finding and researching your topic

LIST OF SUB-TOPICS

- Finding a topic for a term paper
- Finding and using sources
- Doing a periodical search
- Taking and organizing notes

Economists view the world through the lens of efficiency, starting from the assumption that individuals behave rationally and focusing on the problem of allocating scarce resources. From this common analytical perspective, economists study a wide range of topics, involving the behavior of individuals, organizations, and nations. The economic approach can be applied so broadly that choosing a topic to write on can be difficult. Indeed, once you start looking at the world through the eyes of an economist, almost anything can be analyzed in terms of choice under constraint.

Your own research has to meet the terms of the assignment as well as the time and other constraints you face. You may need to read books and journal articles in the library or pore over data sets on a computer. In either case, you will need a topic before you can begin. If your instructor gives you a list of topics, a review of related research may help you choose among them. If the research question is entirely up to you, a literature search is often not the best way to begin. Immersing yourself in the literature before you have found a topic may convince you that all the interesting questions have already been tackled. At the very least, literature searches should be guided by very general topic ideas.

FINDING A TOPIC FOR A TERM PAPER

Though there is no one way to find a topic, thinking of the issues that interest you is a great place to begin. While the range of possible topics is large, there are some well-defined fields in economics, and your own interests are likely to fit into one of these (see Appendix A for an annotated list of fields). Course materials, textbooks, handouts, and so on are obvious and convenient places to look, especially since your topic will most likely have to pertain to the course subject. But reading the newspaper and keeping an eye on current events can be even more helpful. Once you have a general idea, you should go to the literature and see how economists have tried thinking about it.

For example, say your interest is piqued by recent shootings in both schools and workplaces. What role has the availability of guns played in these events? What are the effects of banning guns? Implementing tougher gun control laws? Though this might initially strike you as a government or law project, many of the underlying issues are fundamentally economic – gun control measures explicitly place limits on supply and attempt to put guns in disfavor or reduce demand. Once you have identified guns and gun control as an area of interest, do your literature search (more on this later). Pick out the relevant articles and scour them for content as well as for additional sources. Try to narrow down your topic. Have the authors pointed out any future research areas? Are there any issues that you think have not been fully addressed?

In addition to finding something that interests you, you will also need a project that can be done within the parameters of the assignment (for example, length, due date, access to research materials). If the topic does not interest you, you probably will not put in the effort needed to do a good job or ask the right questions along the way. On the other hand, a profoundly interesting topic may not be manageable given the time and other constraints that you face.

As another example, say you are interested in the stock market and want to know what determines stock prices. From basic economic theory, you know that prices are determined by supply and demand, but what specific relationships do you need to study and what data do you need to gather? You think about it for a while and realize there are many parts to your question. What determines the price of a particular company's stock is a different question from what determines the level of stock prices in general (as measured by Dow Jones or another index), though the two may be related. And what determined stock prices yesterday might be different from what explains changes in stock prices in the future. Each of these questions could be the subject of an interesting paper. Your original topic was overly broad; you should focus on a single, manageable question.

Get started on your research even if you do not have a precise topic; it will evolve along the way. The question you begin with may become less interesting, and something new may draw your attention. You may be persuaded by an argument you encounter or find data that pose a problem you had not considered. You may find no data on one topic and a goldmine on another. Shaping your topic in this way is perfectly fine, but do not get trapped in an endless maze of new, or just slightly revised, topics. You want your search to converge on a manageable topic in a reasonable amount of time. Find a question you can answer and begin your work.

FINDING AND USING SOURCES

All academic writing involves the use of source materials. Archae-ologists look in the ground for artifacts, about which volumes of research may subsequently appear. Biologists look through micro-scopes and write up the laboratory experiments they perform. Historians study documents; sociologists interview subjects . . .

Economic research typically begins with a (large) set of numerical data – say, a list of per capita incomes for every country in the United Nations or the history of daily closing prices for shares of XYZ Corporation over the last year. In these long lists of numbers, economists look for patterns, or regularities, that reveal some underlying relationship between economic variables and help explain how some part of the economy works. A data set could include hundreds or thousands of entries; thus, statistical tools are used to summarize this information and ease your job of communi-cating with your audience. The mean of a large set of numbers conveys important information in a compact form. Knowing the standard deviation and other statistical measures can also be helpful when describing the population under investigation and presenting the results of your research.

Economic sources come in two types. The first is empirical data: facts about the real world that come in, or can be easily converted into, numerical form (for example, prices, quantities, income levels). The second is academic literature: books or articles that you read in the library that can help you organize your ideas and make sense of the heaps of data you have accumulated.

In general you will not have the time or resources to go into the field and compile your own data – administer questionnaires, study individual balance sheets, budgets, etc. Instead, you will rely on others to collect your data, including other economists as well as demographers, auditors, and "official" statisticians. These data are compiled in a number of standard secondary sources, such as the *Economic Report of the President* and the *Statistical Abstract of the United*

States. These volumes and others (see Appendix B2) contain detailed information on public and private spending, wage and tax rates, and work force size and education levels, as well as other information grouped by states, industries, and nations. Economists frequently begin their research with these sources; they will either point you to the proper primary source or contain the precise data you need for your paper.

You will also want to look at academic journals and other scholarly literature on your topic. Using scholarly sources will allow you to invoke the authority of experts in the field to sanction your analysis or to establish the point of departure for your own original contribution. You need to become familiar with what others have thought and written so that you can communicate your findings in terms your audience will recognize. Perhaps you will apply a standard model found in the literature to new evidence or compare two models and see which does a better job explaining the data you have found.

These works will also point you to additional sources. Bibliographies, citations, and footnotes may reveal a single, seminal forerunner. Read it. If you come across a "review" or "survey" article, you have hit the jackpot. It will contain an authoritatively complete summary of the literature in the field.

DOING A PERIODICAL SEARCH

Periodical literature was once indexed in cumbersome hardbound volumes. Nowadays, there are a number of very useful electronic indices available on-line and updated frequently. Most are publicly available on the Internet, although some reside on your institution's proprietary system. Appendix C describes those sources that are used most frequently by economists.

Depending on the service you are using, your search can be very deep, including title, author, and subject as well as abstracts, tables of contents, and related topic fields. This makes electronic searching far more powerful than anything that could be done just a few years ago. Once you find a relevant article, look at the abstract. Check a few more items and retrieve from the shelves whatever looks interesting and useful.

TAKING AND ORGANIZING NOTES

The books, articles, charts, and tables strewn before you are the objects of your research, the evidence you will marshal to support your argument. Your first encounter with your sources should be carefully recorded: you should document your findings and give proper credit to the sources you use.

First, take down the complete bibliographic record:

Author(s) (or Editor(s)).		
Title.		
Journal.	*Volume.*	*Number.*
Date.	*Pages.*	

For the Goldin and Katz (1996) example used in Chapter 1, your notes would look as follows:

Goldin, Claudia and Katz, Lawrence F.
"Technology, Skill and the Wage Structure: Insights from the Past."
American Economic Review, 86 (2).
May 1996. Pp. 252–257.

Keep a file of notes on each article you read. This should include the main points of the article and any important results. Make sure to clearly set off direct quotations by using quotation marks. Avoid paraphrasing, because it will be difficult to separate the original wording from your own later on. You can add your own comments afterwards, but it is important to keep an accurate record of your first encounter with the source.

Taking good notes will accomplish several things. First, you will have all your references at hand when you are writing the paper, so you will not have to go searching for a quote or chart when you are in your dorm room and the article you need is in the library. Second, you will leave a clear record for your readers to follow, so that they can go to the originals for more information or to see the facts for themselves. Finally, you will leave signposts for yourself so that you can know where you have been and separate your own ideas and results from those you found in your sources. This will help you avoid plagiarizing, which can happen inadvertently as your own ideas blur into what you have "learned" from others. The unacknowledged use of another writer's words or ideas is plagiarism, whether intended or not. Poor note taking and sloppy documentation mechanics can lead to plagiarism, but such mistakes are easy to correct and avoid.

Start taking notes right away. A word processor can make things easier, but even if you use pen and paper, try to develop good note-taking habits from the outset. Create a note file for each source you find. Group your notes by topic, alphabetically, chronologically, or otherwise. As you organize them, add comments and summaries, pick out important themes, and focus on issues for further research. These notes should help motivate your project by shaping the analytical model used and, through your summaries, form the beginnings of a good literature review.

Chapter 4

The term paper

LIST OF SUB-TOPICS

- Outlining your paper
- Writing your literature review
- Presenting your hypothesis
- Presenting your results
- Discussing your results

You have chosen your topic, done your research, and settled on your ideas, and now you have to write the paper. If you have done your job properly up to now, you should have a topic, some data, and plenty of notes on things you have read. Now your task is to decide how to focus your question and ideas, assemble the pieces into a structure that hangs together, and present an argument others will find persuasive.

Remember: writing is a process. Start with a few lines, perhaps just section headings, and then build up detail and flesh out your analysis. The key to the process is not to become too rigid too soon. While you want enough structure to get started, you also want to allow the overall shape of your paper to evolve somewhat along the way.

OUTLINING YOUR PAPER

The outline for your term paper is the agenda you set for the things you want to accomplish. A good term paper will ask an interesting question and offer a plausible answer. It should be plausible in that it is (probably) true, but also not obviously or patently true; and it should be supportable in that it is subject to factual observation or logical demonstration (Gordon Harvey, *Harvard Writing Program*).

No matter what your field or topic, there is a fairly standard set of things you want to accomplish in the paper:

INTRODUCTION	pose an interesting question or problem
LITERATURE REVIEW	survey the literature on your topic
METHODS/DATA	formulate your hypothesis and describe your data
RESULTS	present your results with the help of graphs and charts
DISCUSSION	critique your method and/or discuss any policy implications
CONCLUSIONS	summarize what you have done; pose questions for further research

Not every assignment will require all of these parts, but your term paper will impress your reader if you have done a good job on most of them. You might want to write the introduction and conclusions after you have completed the body of the paper. Few points are given for subtlety or surprise. You should prepare your audience for what you are going to do, then do it, then summarize what you have done.

WRITING YOUR LITERATURE REVIEW

Depending on your assignment, preparing a literature review might entail an exhaustive library search or referencing the single paper your instructor has assigned. You should have notes, either on index cards or in files on your computer, on the books and articles you have read. Read over your summaries and comments and begin to look for common themes that can organize your review. What is the main point of the article, and how does it relate to your topic? Do other authors offer a similar position? An opposing one?

As you think through these questions, keep in mind that the literature review has two functions. The first is simply to demonstrate your familiarity with scholarly work on your topic – to provide a *survey* of what you have read, trace the development of important themes, and draw out any tensions in prior research. The second function is to lay the foundations for your paper, to provide *motivation*. The particular issues you intend to raise, the terms you will employ, and the approach you will take should be defined with reference to previous scholarly works. By drawing on such sources, you can find sanction for your own approach and invoke the authority of those who have written on the topic before you.

In some instances, these two functions will pull in opposite directions: the first toward including as many sources as possible, the second toward selecting only those that are useful for your argument. In any case, more research is better than less, and a summary is always selective, insofar as only some things can be included and others left out. The selections you make will necessarily reflect your own interests and, hopefully, lead the reader to take an interest in the argument you will present.

35

FOR EXAMPLE

Martin Feldstein begins his article, "Social Security, Induced Retirement, and Aggregate Capital Accumulation" (1974), with a discussion of the development of economists' thinking on lifetime savings patterns. He starts with a famous early work in the field:

> Ever since Harrod's (1948) discussion of "hump savings," economists have recognized the importance of saving during working years for consumption during retirement (p. 906).

"Hump-savings" refers to the shape of an individual's savings curve over time: low at the beginning, higher in the middle, lower at the end. This basic model is used throughout the paper and holds together all that follows. Feldstein cites a number of authors who have observed this regularity in empirical data on personal savings patterns as confirmation of the model. He goes on to argue that while the "hump-savings" model works well to explain most of the observed data, the effect of certain government policies on individual savings has never been measured empirically. In particular, he poses the question: What is the effect of social security on individuals' lifetime savings? He then cites the work of three other authors as well as his own earlier work as examples of this neglect.

In this way, Feldstein presents his current research as a necessary development out of well established research program, the next question to ask on a line stemming from important ancestors to contemporary scholarly research. The reader is thus prepared for the empirical analysis that follows, which shows that "social security depresses personal savings by 30–50 percent" (Martin Feldstein, 1974).

PRESENTING YOUR HYPOTHESIS

The literature review sets out the issues that motivate your paper and demonstrates your familiarity with what others have written on the topic. The next step is to formulate a specific questions, problem, or conjecture, and to describe the approach you will take to answer, solve, or test it. Often, this will take the form of an empirical hypothesis: "social security depresses personal savings"; "high levels of employment are related to high levels of inflation," etc. An empirical hypothesis makes a claim about how some part of the economy works and can be assessed by analyzing the relevant data.

In presenting your hypothesis, you need to discuss the data set you are using and, in most cases, the type of regression you will run. You should say where you found the data, and use a table, graph, or simple statistics to summarize them. You should explain how the data relate to your hypothesis and note any problems they pose. If you have only a small set of observations, or have to use proxies for data you cannot directly observe, you should explicitly acknowledge this.

FOR EXAMPLE

In "Employment-Based Health Insurance and Job Mobility: Is There Evidence of Job-Lock?," Brigitte Madrian (1994) writes:

To study the phenomenon of job-lock, one would like information on individual and family health status, worker mobility, and the health insurance plans of both the firm for which and individual works and to which one could move. Unfortunately, information on health status and health insurance is not widely available in labor force surveys, information on worker mobility is not typically available in health surveys, and information on insurance plans of companies for which an individual could have worked is nonexistent.

Madrian goes on to offer an alternative method to study job-lock by looking at two groups of workers who are similar in all respects but one: one group has employer provided health insurance and the other does not. She then measures the number of times the workers change jobs and observes a significant negative relationship between employment-based health insurance and job turnover.

Madrian is careful not to jump to a hasty conclusion, noting that this correlation is not itself conclusive evidence of job-lock. Employers that provide health insurance often provide other benefits that will affect mobility. In addition, unobserved characteristics of workers' health status may independently affect job sorting and mobility because workers with pre-existing conditions may have a harder time getting new health insurance. Still, Madrian's careful analysis controls for as many factors as possible and allows her to conclude: "that there is substantial health insurance-related job-lock."

In a term paper, it may not be possible to reach conclusive empirical results. You may have incomplete data, or your regression coefficients may not be significant, or you may not have controlled for significantly all the factors involved. It is better to acknowledge these shortcomings than to make overly broad and unsupported statements.

PRESENTING YOUR RESULTS

by Christopher Foote

One of the more common mistakes made by authors of economic papers is to forget that their results need to be written up as carefully and clearly as any other part of the paper. There are essentially two decisions to make. First, how many empirical results should be presented? Second, how should these results be described in the text?

How many results should I report?

Less is usually more. A common mistake made by virtually all novice researchers (including graduate students) is to include every parameter estimate from every regression specification that was run. Such a "kitchen sink" approach is usually taken to show the world that the researcher has been careful and done a lot of work and that the main results of the paper are not sensitive to the choice of sample period, minor changes in the list of regressors, etc. However, pages of parameter estimates usually muddy the message of the paper. The reader will get either lost or bored. A good general rule is to present only those parameter estimates that speak directly to your topic.

 FOR EXAMPLE

Suppose you are writing about the effect of education on wages. Your main regression places an individual's wage on the left-hand side and regressors such as education, race, gender, seniority at the individual's job, labor market experience, and state of residence on the right hand side. You believe that the regressor of interest (education) is correlated with the error term of the wage equation – more "able" people earn more at their jobs, i.e. have a high residual in the wage equation, and also obtain more education. Because of this correlation between the error term and education, the measured effect of education in the regression will reflect not only the true causal effect of education on wages but also some of the effect of ability on wages. To circumvent this "ability bias" you use a separate measure as a proxy for ability. Though such a proxy is probably not available, assume for the sake of exposition that a special dataset contains an individual's evaluation by his or her second grade teacher. When presenting your results you want to focus only on the estimates of the education effect and the ability effect. Your table might look something like this:

Table I   OLS estimates of the effect of education on wages-
dependent variable: log of yearly earnings
1985–1995

	(1)	(2)	(3)	(4)
Years of education	0.091	0.031	0.086	0.027
	(0.001)	(0.003)	(0.002)	(0.005)
Ability dummy		0.251		0.301
		(0.010)		(0.010)
State dummies included?	No	No	Yes	Yes
No. of obs.	35,001	35,001	19,505	19,505
No. of persons	5,505	5,505	4,590	4,590
Adj. R^2	0.50	0.55	0.76	0.79

Notes: Standard errors are in parentheses. Data are from the Tennessee Second Grade Ability Survey and Wage Follow-up, and include individuals evaluated between 1962 and 1971. The "ability dummy" equals one if the individual's second grade teacher classified the individual as "able," zero otherwise. Each regression also includes yearly dummies, 10 one-digit industry and 20 Census-defined occupation dummies, labor market experience (defined as age −6), experience squared, seniority on the current job, seniority squared, Census region of current residence, marital status, race, gender, and a dummy variable denoting whether the individual lives in a city of more than 100,000 persons. Columns (3) and (4) have fewer observations because state of residence is not available for some individuals.

Note that Table I does not present the parameter estimates of your control variables, regressors such as marital status and seniority, but presents any detail that helps interpret the parameters of interest (including the identification of the dependent variable, which is annoyingly left off of many tables). For example, explain how you define labor market experience as well as why the third and fourth regressions have fewer observations than the first and second regressions. The notes to your table should be extensive enough so that the reader does not have to look back at the text to understand what is being presented. The cardinal sin, to be avoided at all costs, is to report your estimates in terms of "α" or "β" (the actual Greek letters from your equations) without stating what these coefficients mean. Using eight-letter abbreviations from your Stata or SAS program (YEDUCT1 or ABIL25A) is not much better.

Do not worry about repeating yourself in the text and the notes – this will often be necessary so the reader can understand your table without looking back at the text. You should present enough information in total so that a researcher could replicate your results. For very detailed projects, this may require a data appendix. Finally, the notes to the table should indicate whether you are reporting standard errors or t-statistics in the parentheses underneath the coefficients. Both are seen in the literature, so you must be clear which you are using. As a general rule, it is better to report standard errors. That way, your readers can more easily choose the statistical method they would like to use in evaluating your numbers.

After presenting these results you may want to discuss any additional robustness checks that you performed. The third and fourth columns of Table I are robustness checks of sorts; they show that the effect of including ability in the regression is the same whether or not we include state level dummy variables. We may also have checked whether the estimate of the education effect is lower when ability is included, if we subset only on male household heads or if we restrict the sample to the 1990s. Sometimes all that is necessary is to let the reader know in the text that you performed these tests and that the main results were unaffected. For a single robustness check, this information can even appear in a footnote keyed to the relevant portion of the text. If there are many robustness checks however, you may want to present these results in another, more parsimonious table.

How should I describe my empirical results in the text?

After you decide how to make your tables, graphs, and figures, you should clearly and precisely describe them in the text. Establish the main point of the table in the topic sentence of a paragraph. For example, you can describe the above table like this:

> Table I shows that including a measure of ability in the wage equation dramatically lowers the predicted effect of education on earnings. Column 1 does not include an ability measure and indicates that a year of education

> raises wages by 9.1 percent. Column 2 adds the ability measure and the education effect drops to 3.1 percent. Columns 3 and 4 show that this general pattern is repeated even when state level dummy variables are included. The estimates in Table I are therefore consistent with the hypothesis that the OLS estimates suffer from an upward ability bias.

Note that the first and last sentences in this paragraph are "big picture" statements, describing how the results in this table fit into the overall theme of the paper.

Too often, authors do not pay close attention to the paragraphs that describe their results. The results are already in the table. What difference does it make how they are described in the text? The reason to craft these descriptive paragraphs carefully is that any well-designed empirical project is complex; a lot of factors must be considered in order for any single factor to be precisely estimated. You want to guide the reader and focus his or her attention on the important parts of the table, and in the right order. Moreover, no empirical paper turns out perfectly. Usually the data do not resoundingly support each and every idea. In these cases, it is crucial to discuss your results as honestly and carefully as possible.

FOR EXAMPLE

Assume that you are studying the effect of the population share of lawyers in a city on the subsequent growth rate of that city. Your theory says that cities with lots of lawyers will grow more slowly than other cities, but the same is not true of cities with lots of other highly educated professionals, such as doctors. You get data on the population percentage of both doctors and lawyers in 25 cities in 1950 and on the growth rates of these cities as well as the Census region for each city (Mountain, Pacific, Mid-Atlantic, etc.) from 1950 to 1990. Your regression places the 1950–1990 growth rate of the city on the left hand side; the regressor of interest is the "lawyer share" of population. The results are presented in the table below:

Table II   Estimates of the effect of lawyers on city growth
            dependent variable: city's population growth rate,
            1950–1990

	(1)	(2)	(3)
Share of lawyers in population, 1950	−0.09 (0.01)	−0.08 (0.03)	−0.07 (0.05)
Share of doctors in population, 1950		0.05 (0.03)	0.05 (0.05)
Region dummies included?	No	No	Yes
No. of obs.	25	25	25
Adj. R^2	0.10	0.12	0.50

Notes: Standard errors are in parentheses. The shares of doctors and lawyers are taken from the Five Percent Public Use Micro Sample of the 1950 U.S. Census and are defined as the share of each profession among employed persons in the population aged 25–64. A "city" is defined as Standard Metropolitan Statistical Area; constant SMSA definitions are used from 1950 to 1990. Region dummies correspond to the 10 "major regions" as defined by the Census Bureau.

A bad way to write up this table is:

The first column of Table II shows the main effect predicted by theory. The second column shows that doctors do not have the same effect on city growth. Finally, the inclusion of regional dummy variables does not significantly affect the main point estimates, though statistical precision is lost.

A better way to write up the table is like this:

Table II shows that a high share of lawyers in a city's population appears to lead to slower growth. Yet, when all the determinants of city growth (such as Census Region growth) are accounted for, the estimate of this effect becomes less precise. The first column shows that a 10 percentage-point increase in the lawyer share of population decreases the future city growth by about 0.9 percentage points. Column 2 shows that, by contrast, a high doctor share does not lead to lower growth. In fact, the point estimate for the doctor share is positive, though not statistically significant. Note however that the estimates in Column 2 are less precise than those in Table I, as the standard error for the lawyer effect rises from 0.01 to 0.03. Since the doctor and lawyer share are strongly (positively) correlated, multicollinearity reduces the precision of the regression. Statistical precision becomes even more of a concern in Column 3, when we add dummy variables for Census region. The size of the lawyer effect remains about the same (−0.07 compared with −0.09 and −0.08), but adding so many new regressors causes the standard errors to rise to the point that the lawyer effect is statistically indistinguishable from zero. The implication is that lawyers do have a negative effect on city growth but that although the point estimate is robust to the inclusion of other relevant variables it is not precisely estimated because of the small sample size.

The Bottom Line

When writing up your empirical results focus only on what is important and be as clear as possible. You may feel that you are repeating yourself and that the reader may be offended at how closely you are leading him or her through your tables and graphs but, to paraphrase John Kenneth Galbraith, both smart and dumb readers will appreciate your pointing things out directly and clearly. The dumb readers need the help, and the smart ones will take silent pleasure in the knowledge that they did not need your assistance!

DISCUSSING YOUR RESULTS

Many of the topics that interest economists have real world policy implications. Your own research may present strong findings about the effects of existing or proposed policies. While this is fine, you should not conclude that "this should be done" or "this should not be done." You should avoid making value judgments and rely instead on economic facts and analyses. Even when you have reached your own conclusions about which policy is desirable, your reader should be able to consider the facts and make the policy decision for himself or herself.

For example, you may find that substituting policy X for current policy Y would raise GDP by 2 percent. That is an appropriate conclusion in a term paper. Be careful, however, not to simply assert that policy X should be substituted for policy Y. For one thing, it can be very difficult to measure the welfare consequences of a given set of policies. Dollars and cents may be easy to measure, but individuals' well being is not. In addition, your own research may not have accounted for certain distributional issues, legal issues, matters of national sovereignty or any number of other things that ultimately affect the desirability of a given policy.

In the discussion of your result, you should also point out the limitations of your research, say the relatively small number of observations you have or the simplicity of the functional form you have tested. In an undergraduate term paper such limitations are expected. In general, it is better to show your instructor that you understand the limits of your method than make broad claims you do not support. You can also suggest questions or alternative approaches for further research.

Once you have completed the discussion of your results, you can add a short conclusion summarizing what you have done. Then go back and write an introduction that provides a roadmap for the reader. If you have budgeted your time, you should have a chance to revise the paper, with the goal of achieving greater clarity. Finally, ask a friend to proofread your work. Make necessary corrections and then submit.

Chapter 5

Formatting and documentation

by Kerry Walk

LIST OF SUB-TOPICS

- Placing citations in your paper
- Listing your references
- Three types of sources
- Basic guidelines
- Sample entries

Citing the sources you use when you write a paper in economics is a matter of honesty, credibility, and courtesy. When you indicate to your reader that a fact or theory derives from a source, you are being honest by giving credit where it is due, i.e., not falsely claiming to have originated the fact or theory yourself. You are gaining credibility by showing your readers that you have done your research. And you are behaving courteously by letting your readers know where they can find the same information, in case they want to do further reading on the topic.

There is no standard style of acknowledging sources in economics papers, but a good model to emulate is the style used in one of the field's most influential journals: *The American Economic Review*. We will call this the AER documentation style. Use this style when you write an economics paper in which you have cited one or more sources.

> *The American Economic Review*: style guide
> http://www.aeaweb.org/aer/styleguide.html
>
> *The American Economic Review*: sample references
> http://www.aeaweb.org/aer/sampleref.html

In the AER style, writers briefly indicate sources in the text of the paper and provide fuller bibliographical information in a REFERENCES section at the end of the paper. Footnotes are reserved for such substantive matters as suggestions for further reading, an elaboration of a point, an interesting but not germane rebuttal of a source's opinion, and so on.

PLACING CITATIONS IN YOUR PAPER

When deriving a theory or fact from a source, cite the source in the text of your paper. Your in-text citation will contain the name of the author(s) and the year of publication. The way this information is formatted depends on (1) whether you wish to draw attention to the source and (2) whether you have referred to the author(s) previously in your paper.

Loud reference

If you wish to acknowledge the source of an idea explicitly, cite the name of the author(s) in the body of your sentence and place the publication date in parentheses. The first time you cite the name of the author(s), provide both first and last names:

Vincent P. Crawford and Hans Haller (1990).

Thereafter, refer to the author(s) by last name only:

Crawford (1998).

Thus, a first-time reference:

Sender–receiver games, introduced by Jerry Green and Nancy Stokey (1980) and Vincent P. Crawford and Joel Sobel (1982), provide the simplest stylized environment in which communication is essential.

A reference to authors previously mentioned:

These theories come in two guises: explicit dynamic theories, i.e., Canning (1992) and Nöldeke and Samuelson (1992), and static solution concepts, i.e., Blume et al. (1993) and Wärneryd (1993).

- Use "et al." (et alias = and others) when authors number three or more.
- Place punctuation, if any is called for, after the parenthetical date.

Soft reference

To evoke a source that substantiates a claim you make, cite the name of the author(s), as well as the date, in parentheses. As above, the first time you cite the author(s), provide both first and last names:

> (Vincent P. Crawford and Hans Haller, 1990; Matthew Rabin and Joel Sobel, 1996)

Thereafter, refer to the author(s) by last name only:

> (Crawford and Sobel, 1982; Crawford, 1998)

- Authors are listed in order of publication date.
- Separate sources with a semi-colon.

Thus, in an article that has already cited Andreas Blume:

> Such "babbling equilibria" are proper (Roger B. Myerson, 1978; Blume, 1994), and even strategic stability (Elon Kohlberg and Jean-Francois Mertens, 1986) does not rule out uninformative equilibria in general.

LISTING YOUR REFERENCES

When readers want to know more about a source – what its title is, where it was published, when it appeared – they will look at your list of REFERENCES at the end of your paper. The bibliographical information there makes it possible for readers themselves to track down the source.

Note that the word REFERENCES is capitalized – because AER style demands that it be so. Indentation, capitalization, punctuation, and the ordering of information in REFERENCES define a particular documentation style and should be scrupulously followed. Even boldface, italics, and spacing count.

THREE TYPES OF SOURCES

The information contained in a REFERENCES entry and the way in which this information is formatted depend largely on the type of source it is. Is the source an article in a journal? a reference work? a book by a single author? an essay in a collection? a working paper? an unpublished doctoral dissertation? In order to format the entry correctly, you need to know.

There are three main types of sources: journal articles, books, and unpublished sources.

Journal articles	Appear in publications that are issued at regular intervals, or periods; hence "periodical," the synonym for "journal." A telltale sign of the journal is the publication date: month (or season) and year. Another sign is the absence of a publisher's name (such as "Cambridge University Press").
Book	The opening pages will give such information as author (if there is one), title, name of the publisher, and place and year of publication. A book that is a collection of essays (also known as an "anthology") will give the name(s) of its editor(s) and will feature a Table of Contents listing the essays in the collection. Such a collection should not be confused with a periodical.

| Unpublished sources | Available from the individuals who wrote them or the institution that sponsored them, they are of various kinds: the mimeograph (a photocopied paper or report), the unpublished doctoral dissertation, the working paper, and so on. Other unpublished sources include course lectures, websites, and e-mail messages. |

BASIC GUIDELINES

Whether a source is a journal article, a book, or an unpublished source, you should follow these basic guidelines when formatting it for your REFERENCES.

Alphabetical listing

Sources are listed in alphabetical order, according to the last name of the author (or the last name of the primary author, if there's more than one). If the source has no author – for example, U.S. Bureau of the Census – it should be listed alphabetically according to its initial letter.

Formatting author(s)' names

Authors' last names are always listed before their first names. The punctuation separating individual authors' names changes depending on the number of authors.

One author:
Davis, Donald R.

Two authors:
Kohlberg, Elon and Mertens, Jean-Francois.

Three authors:
Kandori, Michihiro; Mailath, George J. and Rob, Rafael.

Four authors:
Berg, Joyce E.; Daley, Lane; Dickhaut, John and O'Brien, John.

■ Note the semi-colon (;) used to divide some, but not all, of the names in the three- and four-author examples.

Repeat authors

Sometimes your REFERENCES will contain more than one source by the same author or authors. In this case, do not spell out the author's or authors' name(s) after the first entry; instead, use an underscore (____) to signify the name(s). List sources by the same author(s) in order of publication date.

Krugman, Paul R. and Venables, Anthony J. "Integration and the Competitiveness of Peripheral Industry," in Christopher Bliss and Jorge Braga de Macedo, eds., *Unity with diversity in the European economy*, Cambridge: Cambridge University Press, 1990, pp. 56–77.

> _____. "Globalization and the Inequality of Nations." *Quarterly Journal of Economics*, November 1995, *110* (4), pp. 857–80.

- Note that the second source above was written by exactly the same authors as the first source. If the second source had been written by Krugman and, say, Young, their names would have to have been spelled out.
- If the second source had been a book written during the same year (1990) as the first source, the first source would be listed as 1990a, the second as 1990b.

Inclusive page numbers

Page numbers are inclusive – that is, they refer to the pages on which the entire source may be found, not just the page or two from which you drew a fact or theory.

- If the first and last page numbers share an initial numeral, drop the initial numeral of the last page number: for example, pp. 367–98 (and not pp. 367–398).

SAMPLE ENTRIES

When formatting your REFERENCES section, use the following sample entries as models. If you don't find the type of source you are looking for, pick up a copy of the *American Economic Review* in your school's library and try to find a model there, or emulate the closest approximation you can find.

Article published in a journal

An entry for a journal article will contain the following information, formatted as you see:

> **Author.** "Title of the Article." *Name of the Journal,* Month Year, *Issue Numeral* (Issue Number), pp. X–Z.

- Note the boldfaced author name and the italicized journal name and issue numeral.
- The "pp." stands for "page numbers."
- The second line is indented, as are all lines after the first one.

No author

> **Economist.** "The Economist Survey of China." November 28, 1992, *325* (7787), pp. 1–22.

One author

> **Davis, Donald R.** "Intra-Industry Trade: A Heckscher–Ohlin–Ricardo Approach." *Journal of International Economics,* November 1995, *39* (3–4), pp. 201–26.

Two authors

> **Kohlberg, Elon and Mertens, Jean-Francois.** "On the Strategic Stability of Equilibrium." *Econometrica,* September 1986, *54* (5), pp. 1003–37.

Three authors

> **Kandori, Michihiro; Mailath, George J. and Rob, Rafael.** "Learning, Mutation, and Long-Run Equilibria in Games." *Econometrica*, January 1993, *61* (1), pp. 29–56.

Four authors

> **Berg, Joyce E.; Daley, Lane; Dickhaut, John and O'Brien, John.** "Controlling Preferences for Lotteries on Units of Experimental Exchange." *Quarterly Journal of Economics*, May 1986, *101* (2), pp. 281–306.

Books

In its most basic form, a book will contain the following information, formatted as you see:

> **Author.** *The title of the book.* City of Publication: Name of the Press, Year of Publication.

- Note the boldfaced author name and the italicized title.
- Only the initial letter of the title is capitalized.
- The second line is indented, as are all lines after the first one.

Reference works

> **U.S. Bureau of the Census, Department of Commerce.** *U.S. census of manufactures.* Washington, DC: U.S. Government Printing Office, 1992.

> National Science Foundation/Division of Science Resource Studies. *Research and development in industry.* Washington, DC: U.S. Government Printing Office, 1992.

■ Even the period after **"Studies"** is in boldface.

By a single author

> Rosenberg, Nathan. *Perspectives on technology.* New York: Cambridge University Press, 1976.
> Helpman, Elhanan and Krugman, Paul R. *Market structure and foreign trade.* Cambridge, MA: MIT Press, 1985.

■ MA, the abbreviation for "Massachusetts," is used with "Cambridge" to avoid confusion with the first Cambridge – Cambridge, England.

An essay in an edited collection

> Whinnom, Keith. "Linguistic Hybridization and the Special Case' of Pidgins and Creoles," in Dell Hymes, ed., *Pidginization and creolization of languages.* Cambridge: Cambridge University Press, 1971, pp. 91–116.
> Krugman, Paul R. and Venables, Anthony J. "Integration and the Competitiveness of Peripheral Industry," in Christopher Bliss and Jorge Braga de Macedo, eds., *Unity with diversity in the European economy.* Cambridge: Cambridge University Press, 1990, pp. 56–77.

> **Maskus, Keith.** "Comparing International Trade Data and Product and National Characteristics Data for the Analysis of Trade Models," in Peter Hooper and J. David Richardson, eds., *International economic transactions: Issues in measurement and empirical research.* NBER Studies in Income and Wealth, Vol. 55. Chicago: University of Chicago Press, 1991, pp. 17–56.

- The name of the essay is in quotation marks. Note the capitalization scheme.
- An editor is "ed.," editors are "eds."
- Inclusive page numbers help the reader easily locate the essay.

Unpublished sources

Unpublished Ph.D. dissertation

> **Clausing, Kimberly A.** "Essays in International Economic Integration." Ph.D. dissertation, Harvard University, 1996.

Working paper or discussion paper

> **Kramarz, Francis.** "When Repeated Cheap Talk Generates a Common Language." Working paper, Institut National de la Statistique et des Etudes Economiques (INSEE), 1992.
>
> **Sopher, Barry and Zapater, Iñigo.** "Communication and Coordination in Signalling Games: An Experimental Study." Working paper, Rutgers University, 1994.
>
> **Wei, Shang-Jin.** "How Reluctant Are Nations in Global Integration?" National Bureau of Economic Research (Cambridge, MA) Working Paper No. 5531, April 1996.

Green, Jerry and Stokey, Nancy. "A Two-Person Game of Information Transmission." Harvard Institute of Economic Research Discussion Paper No. 751, Harvard University, 1980.

Mimeograph (i.e. photocopied material)

Fujita, Masahisa; Krugman, Paul R. and Venables, Anthony J. "Agricultural Transport Costs." Mimeo, MIT, December 14, 1996.

Class lecture or speech

Foote, Christopher L. "Introduction to Economic Theory." Lecture in Economics 970, Harvard University, 12 February 1999.

Website

U.S. Census Bureau. http://www.census.gov/ cited 21 February 1999.

E-mail message

Neugeboren, Robert. neugebor@fas.harvard.edu "Economic Models." Personal e-mail, 16 January 1999.

Appendices

APPENDIX A: FIELDS IN ECONOMICS[1]

The economic approach is applicable to a wide range of social interactions, which can make finding a topic for your paper particularly
difficult. Perhaps your instructor has provided a list of potential
topics. Which should you choose? Perhaps the assignment leaves the
choice of a topic entirely up to you. How should you get started?
Below you will find a list of fields in economics that should help
narrow the scope of your choices.

Comparative/reform economics

Now that the Cold War is over, interest in reform economics is on the
rise. Today, many nations around the world are trying to shift from
economic systems based on hierarchical principles of command and
control to market systems based on the principles of free exchange
and competition. Comparative economic systems attempt to explore,
using pertinent theoretical models where possible, how "socialist"
economic life has been organized in practice. Particular attention is
paid to the development strategies pursued and the actual function-
ing of economic arrangements, as well as the balance between plans,

1 Adapted from "A Guide to the Undergraduate Economics Program at
Harvard," R. Neugeboren and A. Mortimer, editors, 1997.

bureaucracies, and informal sectors. Why did "planned" economies appear to function effectively for so long? Why did so many suddenly conclude at the end of the 1980s that they had failed? What, precisely, is wrong with trying to organize economic life on the hierarchical principles of command and control? How can these countries make the transition to market-based systems without undermining the political stability needed to implement reforms?

Development

Annual per capita income in the United States today is $24,000, while half the world's population subsists on less than $1,500 a year. Economists and others have long tried to understand the factors contributing to this enormous gap between rich and poor nations and have long sought effective ways to accelerate growth in developing economies. Over the past thirty years, development economics as a field has dealt with the specific economic problems of relatively poor countries. Understanding development means understanding the political and social conditions that impel and constrain it. For instance, fear of Western imperialism led the rulers of Meiji Japan to overthrow the Tokugama Shogunate and embark on an ambitious economic program that turned medieval Japan into a nineteenth-century industrial power in two generations. In Africa, perhaps most acutely, it is difficult to understand cycles of growth without an appreciation of political patterns and customs. Today, most development economists apply the standard analytical tools of economics to the specific problems confronting developing countries, modifying those tools where necessary.

Environmental economics

Few areas of economics have grown so rapidly in recent years as environmental economics. As people have more fully realized that important natural resources are in finite supply, attempts to conserve and to recycle have steadily gained momentum. Since very few questions of environmental policy can be cast purely in terms of black and white, economists, with their long tradition of analyzing trade-offs, have played important roles in designing environmental regulations. Questions asked include: Does it make most sense to reduce pollution by setting emission standards or through using tax policy to create incentives for emissions reductions? How can we decide which species have the greatest priority for protection? What does "sustainability" consist of?

Economic history

It is hard to gain a coherent picture of what the economy is without understanding how it evolved and what history teaches us about how different economies function. It is important to learn about qualitative and quantitative consequences of the industrial revolution for levels of wealth, the sectoral distribution of production, the distribution of income, the state of technology, the role of government, and the development of commerce. It is important to learn which of current economic institutions and behavioral relationships have persisted over long stretches of time and which are relatively new. It is also important to be exposed to the wide range of past economic problems, so they can know how standard micro and macro techniques apply, and where they fail. Things change, but it can look as if the institutions and practices of today have existed forever. A historical perspective can help bring the issues of today into better focus, just as it can help explain events in the past and offer a trajectory toward the future.

Finance

Robert Merton and Myron Scholes won the 1997 Nobel Prize in Economics for their options pricing model, a relatively simple equation that spawned the field of financial economics. Financial

65

economics studies the behavior and structure of financial markets and institutions, including commercial banks, insurance companies, investment banks, mutual funds – players in the stock and bond markets. Some research focuses on corporate finance and the capital structure of firms, the kinds of analyses that go on inside a corporate finance department of a Wall Street investment bank. Others look at portfolio management and the analysis of risk, arbitrage, and time discounting applied to the valuation of various financial assets. Financial economics has taken on an increasingly international perspective, comparing the financial systems of the USA, Germany, and Japan, for instance, or analyzing the links between the development of local capital markets and the real economy.

Game theory

In the last twenty-five or so years, theorists have made great advances in characterizing the behavior of households, workers, and firms. Among the most active areas of current research are considerations of the roles of imperfect information, uncertainty, and strategic behavior in shaping the way that many economic interactions take place. Game theory is often used for such analyses. These lines of research have been helpful in explaining situations in which, for example, involuntary unemployment is persistent or people cannot get loans despite being willing to pay the going interest rate.

Industrial organization

Industrial organization seeks to apply economic theories of markets to actual industries and firms in the United States and other developed industrial economies. The inquiry starts by comparing the motives and organizations of actual enterprises to those that economic models assume the firm possesses. The industrial organization field is built around a structure–conduct–performance framework.

The constraints imposed on firms by their environments and their competitors lead them to certain strategic choices and activities, which have impacts on the performance of markets as social allocation devices. Research in industrial organization proceeds along two lines: statistical investigations (to make sure that the cases cited are representative) and case studies (to make sure that statistical investigations are really asking the right questions and producing meaningful answers). It is less business-oriented than policy- and theory-oriented – although the analyses of industrial organization hold considerable relevance for those planning business careers.

International economics

Both historically and today the field of international economics has been and is policy-oriented: What should governments do? How should they regulate the cross-border economic relationships that their citizens enter into? As world trade and finance becomes more salient, international economics threatens to become coterminous with the study of economic policy in general. Today, even in such a large economy as the United States, it is very difficult to examine issues in public finance, macroeconomics, industrial organization, or labor economics without paying very close attention to the international context.

Labor economics

Labor economics applies basic tools of microeconomics to the analysis of labor markets and the determination of the wage rate. What are the arguments for and against a minimum wage? What factors explain wage differentials? It distinguishes itself by two features. First, it is an intensely empirical sub-field, in which students are expected to analyze data – often from very large computerized data sets – as part of their study. Second, it is one of the few subfields where actual empirical fieldwork – visits to companies and unions –

is encouraged. Labor economics requires a good knowledge of price theory and a sound grasp of statistics.

Monetary and fiscal policy

The two principal ways that public policy affects the course of the economy in the United States are the government's monetary policy – implemented in financial markets by the country's central bank, the Federal Reserve – and fiscal policy, implemented through the taxing and spending decisions that Congress and the President make (or fail to make). Politicians assume, and economists believe, that such monetary and fiscal policies can exert very strong influences on such determinants of economic welfare as the rate of inflation, the rate of the economy's growth, the level of employment, and ultimately the standard of living.

Public finance

Topics stressed in this field include efficiency and equity arguments for government "interference" in market economies, what it means for the government to provide a level playing field on which private economic activity can take place, theories advanced to explain actual choices by representative governments, the effects of government tax and expenditure decisions on the allocation of resources, and the distribution of well-being. Special attention is given to the fiscal institutions of the United States.

Urban economics

The phrase "urban crisis" is again found on the pages of major news-papers, often linked to issues of poverty, crime, and the breakdown of the family. Detroit has lost more than half its population in the past thirty years. Poverty, crime in inner-city neighborhoods, infra-structure, racial discrimination, friction between immigrant and other ethnic groups; and the gap between the desires for public services and the willingness to pay for them play an even more important role in the American drama today than they did in the late 1960s when studying urban problems was at a fore. Many urban problems have their roots in market processes. Space or location plays a central role in urban markets both in creating value and in generating positive and negative externalities. Ease of transportation is a good, but nearness to high-crime areas is a bad. Open space is a good, but long commutes are a bad. And so forth. You get what you pay for. But you rarely pay for what you(r actions lead other people to) get.

 ## APPENDIX B: ECONOMICS ON THE INTERNET

A wealth of economics-related information is available on the Internet.

Nearly every major institution doing economic research has a website, and much of the data they collect or analysis they produce is available online. Often this information can be accessed for free, though sometimes you may have to register, or pay a fee. When major proprietary datasets are available only for a fee, abridged versions of these may be available for free, or there may be a free trial period, especially for students. Articles produced by one source may be available via another website; use a search engine to find these items. If the information you seek is mentioned on the website, but there are no direct links, see if there is a Web contact you can email. In addition, there are thousands of secondary websites that offer significant economic data and analyses that are easy to access, and they often provide links to where you can get more material. Use an internet search engine such as Google (www.google.com) to find these items.

Internet data generally come in four forms: as a Web page (*.html) that you can save, as an Adobe Acrobat file (*.pdf) that you can download, as regular files (*.doc, *.xls, etc.) that you can also download, and as data sets. With large datasets, you download not simply a file but the actual data series from another computer, and you have a choice of format (*.txt, *.csv, *.xls, etc.). Excel is a common choice, though if you are going to use this data in a statistical package, find out which format your application will accept, as converting from one version to another is usually complicated.

This appendix has two sections. The first section, "B1: Economics links," is a brief directory of useful websites that contain links to hundreds of other sites, covering much of the universe of economics on the World Wide Web. The second section, "B2: Statistical sources," provides information on where to obtain quantitative data, either in a library or on the Web. If you know what data you want and where to find it, go directly to B2. Otherwise, and in general to familiarize yourself with the world of economics via the Web, start from B1.

 ## APPENDIX B1: ECONOMICS LINKS

American Economic Association www.vanderbilt.edu/AEA is a major organization of academic, business, and government economists, and publishes the *American Economic Review*, *Journal of Economic Literature*, and *Journal of Economic Perspectives*. It has a useful Directory of Members www. vanderbilt.edu/AEA/Directory_Archives.htm, a Job Openings for Economists page www.aeaweb.org/joe, and the Resources for Economists on the Internet site (see below).

Resources for Economists on the Internet (RFE) www. aeaweb.org/ RFE is the comprehensive central directory of information on economics on the Web, listing over 1,500 resources with descriptions, organized into nearly 100 sections. Start from the Abridged Table of Contents www.aeaweb.org/RFE/ssc.html, and in particular check out these sections: Data; Dictionaries,

Glossaries & Encyclopedias; Forums, Mailing Lists & Usenet; and, Other Internet Guides. This site is very useful for finding data relevant to a new research project.

WebEc www.helsinki.fi/WebEc is a broader array of free business and economic resources, and with RFE comprise the WWW Virtual Library in Economics. Of special interest to economics writers are the List of Economics Journals www.helsinki.fi/WebEc/journals.html, and the General Economics Resources, Economics Data, and the individual economics fields' sections.

NetEc netec.wustl.edu/NetEc.html is another useful directory of economics via electronic media, and includes the Information on Printed Papers on BibEc netec.wustl.edu/BibEc.html and Information on Working Papers on WoPEc netec.wustl.edu/WoPEc.html sites.

Some other websites of general interest are:

Yahoo Search of Economics
dir.yahoo.com/Social_Science/economics

Economics Departments, Institutes and Research Centers
netec.wustl.edu/EDIRC/usa.html

Home Pages of Economics Departments in the United States
www.amosweb.com/econdept

Harvard Economics Department's links page
post.economics.harvard.edu/info/links.html

Economic Journals on the Web
www.oswego.edu/~economic/journals.htm

The Information Economy
www.sims.berkeley.edu/resources/infoecon

The Internet Site for Economists (Inomics)
www.inomics.com/cgi/show

World Economic Forum
www.weforum.org

World Trade Organization
www.wto.org

 APPENDIX B2: STATISTICAL SOURCES

A. Secondary sources

The Economic Report of the President

Published annually, this includes: (1) current and foreseeable trends in and annual goals for employment, production, real income, and Federal budget outlays; (2) employment objectives for significant groups of the labor force; and (3) a program for carrying out these objectives. Reports from 1995–2004 are available on the Web at w3.access.gpo.gov/eop.

Statistical Abstract of the United States

Published annually, this is a collection of statistics on social and economic conditions in the United States. Selected international data are also included. It is your best source of information on relevant primary data sources available from the Census Bureau, other Federal agencies, and private organizations. The 1995–2000 Statistical Abstract is available on the Web at www.census.gov/prod/www/statistical-abstract-us.html.

Economic Indicators

Published monthly, this is prepared for the Joint Economic Committee by the Council of Economic Advisors and provides economic information on prices, wages, production, business activity, purchasing power, credit, money and Federal finance. Data from April 1995 forward are available for downloading at www.gpoaccess.gov/indicators/index.html.

World Development Indicators

Published annually by the World Bank, this is a significant compilation of data about development, and is thus a key reference for international comparisons. It includes about 800 indicators in 87 tables, organized in 6 sections, covering 152 countries, 14 country groups, and basic indicators for a further 55 economies. A smaller set of 54 indicators with five years of data (1998–2002) is available free online at devdata.worldbank.org/data-query.

International Financial Statistics

Published by the International Monetary Fund, this is a major source of financial statistics for over 200 countries and areas. The time series data starts from 1948 and provides data at the Country level and World level, detailed global Commodity Prices, as well as information on specific "Economic Concepts." Limited free access is available at ifs.apdi.net.

Country Briefings

This brief data set on about 60 major countries is published by the Economist Intelligence Unit of the *Economist* magazine. This is useful for a quick and easy to understand summary of a country's economic status, and for making simple comparisons between countries. The information is often enough for basic papers and is a good launching point for more in-depth research. Check it out at www.economist.com/countries.

B. Primary sources

Census

Conducted every ten years, the census serves as a vital statistical database. It collects information on an individual's place of birth, ethnicity, native language, family history, annual income, etc., and thus gives a picture of who is living in the United States.
Go to www.census.gov.

Consumer Expenditure Survey (CES)

Conducted since 1889, the CES obtains data on frequently pur-
chased items, such as food or housekeeping supplies, as well as on
major items of expense, such as property or vehicle purchases. This
is a key source of consumption data.
Go to www.bls.gov/cex/home.htm.

Current Population Survey (CPS)

A monthly survey of about 50,000 households, the CPS has been
conducted since 1968. It is the primary source of information on the
characteristics of the United States labor force. In addition to
providing estimates of employment, unemployment, earnings, and
hours of work by occupation, industry, and class of worker, it also
sheds light on a variety of demographic characteristics including
age, sex, race, marital status, and educational attainment of the
labor force. Supplemental questions provide information on a
variety of topics, including school enrollment, income, previous
work experience, health, employee benefits, and work schedules.
Go to www.bls.census.gov/cps/cpsmain.htm.

National Longitudinal Survey (NLS)

The NLS currently provides six panels of information about the
labor market experiences and other aspects of the interviewees. The
surveys also include data about a wide range of events such as
schooling and career transitions, marriage and fertility, training
investments, child-care usage, and drug and alcohol use. The breadth
of these surveys allows for analysis of a variety of topics such as the
transition from school to work, job mobility, youth unemployment,
educational attainment, and the returns to education, welfare
recipiency, the impact of training, and retirement decisions.
Go to www.bls.gov/nls/home.htm.

C. General sources

Bureau of Labor Statistics, stats.bls.gov, reports on a diverse set of indicators including unemployment, the consumer price index as well as lesser known data on work stoppage, collective bargaining, occupational injury, and illness rates, etc.

Bureau of Economic Analysis, www.bea.doc.gov, an agency of the Department of Commerce, provides data on GDP, industrial output and investment as well as international trade.

Fedstats www.fedstats.gov makes public data from over 70 different federal agencies. Data cover such diverse issues as natural resources and the environment, motor vehicle accidents, and wages and weekly earnings.

Federal Reserve Economic Database (FRED) research.stlouisfed. org/fred2 provides historical US economic and financial data, including daily US interest rates, monetary and business indicators, exchange rates, balance of payments, and regional economic data for Arkansas, Illinois, Indiana, Kentucky, Mississippi, Missouri, and Tennessee.

Harvard-MIT Data Center www.hmdc.harvard.edu, the universities' official representative to ICPSR, the Roper Center for Public Opinion Research, and the National Center for Health Statistics (NCHS), provides access to Murray Center and Social Sciences Program Data and is a central contact point for many other archives and data suppliers.

Inter-University Consortium for Political and Social Research (ICPSR) www.icpsr.umich.edu. ICPSR culls a wide variety of data on topics as diverse as education, aging, mental health, criminal justice, etc. It is an invaluable source of on-line data.

National Bureau of Economic Research www.nber.org/data_index. html provides a wide variety of both current and historical macro, industry-level, and individual data. Their listings include the CPS and extracts from the CES.

APPENDIX C: ELECTRONIC INDICES TO PERIODICAL LITERATURE

EconLit

The primary index to economic periodical articles, EconLit is an indexed bibliography with selected abstracts of the economics literature produced by the American Economic Association. It covers over 400 major journals as well as articles in collected volumes, books, book reviews, dissertations, and working papers licensed from the Cambridge University Press Abstracts of Working Papers in Economics. This database must be accessed via a member institution such as a university.

NBER Working Papers

The NBER's website indexes the working papers of affiliated faculty. This is an excellent source for empirical work in progress. Full copies of working papers are available free to subscribers and for a small fee to others from the website or through the mail. They are also available in many academic libraries. Searches are possible at papers.nber.org/papers.

RePEC (Research Papers in Economics)

This website calls itself a "decentralized database of working papers, journal articles and software components," and covers 138,000 working papers and 144,000 journal articles. Searches can be made at www.repec.org.

Social Science Research Network (SSRN)

The SSRN Electronic Library has an Abstract Database containing abstracts on nearly 77,000 scholarly working papers and forthcoming papers and an Electronic Paper Collection currently containing almost 53,000 downloadable full-text documents. It includes working papers from the NBER as well as economics departments around the country. Searches can be made at papers.ssrn.com/sol3/search.taf.

Statistical Universe

A bibliographic database that indexes and abstracts the statistical content of selected US federal and state government publications, state as well as business and association publications. The abstracts include a detailed description of a publication's statistical contents and primary bibliographic information. This database must be accessed via a member institution such as a university.

JSTOR (Journal storage)

Many of the articles you will need are available on-line through JSTOR. JSTOR holds 13 of the top economics journals as well as numerous others in political science, demography, history, and statistics. This database must be accessed via a member institution such as a university.

PAIS

The Public Affairs Information Service International bibliographic index with abstracts includes articles on a complete range of political, social, and public policy issues. This database must be accessed via a member institution such as a university.

References

Camerer, Colin F. and Thaler, Richard H. "Ultimatums, Dictators and Manners." *Journal of Economic Perspectives*, Spring 1995, *9* (2), pp. 209–20.

Feldstein, Martin. "Social Security, Induced Retirement, and Aggregate Capital Accumulation." *Journal of Political Economy*, September–October 1974, *82* (5), pp. 905–26.

Freeman, Richard B. and Hall, Brian. "Permanent Homelessness in America?" in R. B. Freeman, ed., *Labor markets in action: Essays in empirical economics*. Cambridge, MA and London: Harvard University Press, 1989, pp. 134–56.

Gibaldi, Joseph. *MLA handbook for writers of research papers*. New York: Modern Language Association of America, 2003.

Goldin, Claudia and Katz, Lawrence F. "Technology, Skill, and the Wage Structure: Insights from the Past." *American Economic Review*, May 1996, *86* (2), pp. 252–57.

Griliches, Zvi. "Capital–Skill Complementarity." *Review of Economics and Statistics*, November 1969, *51* (4), pp. 465–68.

McCloskey, Donald. "Economical Writing." *Economic Inquiry*, April 1985, *23* (2), pp. 187–222.

Madrian, Brigitte C. "Employment-Based Health Insurance and Job Mobility: Is There Evidence of Job-Lock?" *The Quarterly Journal of Economics,* February 1994, *109* (1), pp. 27–54.

Mankiw, Gregory N. *Principles of economics*. New York: The Dryden Press, 1997.

Popkin, Samuel L. *The rational peasant: The political economy of rural society in Vietnam*. Berkeley, CA: University of California Press, 1979.

Robbins, Lionel. *The nature and significance of economic science*. London: Macmillan Press, 1984.

Strunk, William Jr. and White, E. B. *The elements of style*. New York: Macmillan Press, 1979.

Turabian, Kate L. *A manual for writers of term papers, theses, and dissertations*. Chicago, IL: University of Chicago Press, 1996.

Index